WHAT WOULD A
Holy Woman DO?

WHAT WOULD A
Holy Woman DO?

WENDY WATSON NELSON

DESERET
BOOK

Salt Lake City, Utah

AND YE MUST PRACTISE VIRTUE AND
HOLINESS BEFORE ME CONTINUALLY.

—Doctrine and Covenants 46:33

Library of Congress Cataloging-in-Publication Data
Nelson, Wendy Watson, 1950– author.
    What would a holy woman do? / Wendy Watson Nelson.
        pages cm
    Includes bibliographical references.
    Summary: Author shares positive examples resulting from asking a number of her friends to participate in a three-day challenge to evaluate their life and actions by asking the question "What would a holy woman do?"
    ISBN 978-1-60907-465-4 (hardbound : alk. paper)
    1. Mormon women—Conduct of life.   2. Holiness—Church of Jesus Christ of Latter-day Saints.   I. Title.
    BX8643.W66N45 2013
    248.8'430882893—dc23   2013000968

Printed in the United States of America
Publishers Printing, Salt Lake City, UT

HOLINESS TO THE LORD

Let me begin with a story—a true story. In November of 2007, my husband, Elder Russell M. Nelson, was asked to rededicate the remodeled temple in Tonga. In preparation for the rededication, we walked through the temple so my husband could assess if the remodeling had been completed as requested. Upon close inspection, everything looked perfect. However as we walked out of the temple, we noticed something was missing—something which would prevent the rededication of the temple.

Specific words are placed upon every temple, written in the local language. The words are "House of the Lord, Holiness to the Lord." However, on the Nuku'alofa Tonga Temple that day, those words were missing. What had happened? My husband gently pointed out the omission, the vital words were placed, and the rededication occurred on schedule, November 4, 2007.

On our return to Salt Lake City, Utah, and for several months following, I reflected on that situation and especially on the words "Holiness to the Lord." Just imagine that without those words on the temple, it could not be dedicated to the Lord!

I started to wonder about holiness—the meaning of the word, the placement of those words. I asked myself what I needed to change in my life so that I could have those words—*Holiness to the Lord*—placed upon my life. I wondered if I could ever be worthy to have those words placed upon my life. And if those words *were* placed, what would that mean?

The concept of holiness seemed so lofty, so impossible. Holiness? Me? What did holiness even mean? I knew that "holiness" was not a word I used a lot. I could go many days, sometimes weeks, and never even say the word. How could I start exploring the concept of holiness?

AN E-MAIL INVITATION

I e-mailed six friends and asked for their help. Here is part of the message I wrote to them:

> In thinking about how to learn about holiness, I'm wondering if for three days you would be willing to, just once each day, purposely choose one of your daily activities and try to "be holy" while doing it, or do it as a holy woman would do it. For example, how would a holy woman start her day? What would be on her "to do" list? How would a holy woman approach a difficult assignment or a new overwhelming project? How would she read to a child, or exercise? How would she

talk with a friend, or shop, or play, or pray, or do laundry?

How would a holy woman handle a conflict or avoid a conflict? What would she read, or say, or listen to, or watch, or wear? What would she do in really difficult situations? If someone said something to her that was confusing, or hurtful, or demoralizing, how would a holy woman respond? What would she do? If she were betrayed, or misunderstood, or falsely accused, what would a holy woman do?

How would a holy woman respond to her own success or failure? How would she respond to the successes and failures of others? How would a holy woman use her time and energy and money? How would she prepare to partake of the sacrament each Sunday?

How would a holy married woman welcome her husband home? Or how would she help him to welcome her home so they both felt loved, adored, wanted, and needed? How would a holy single young woman date, or use her time when not dating?

Would you be willing to try that? Choose one thing a day for three days—a different thing each day or the same thing—you can't do this wrong.

My six friends, from the ages of 26 to 65, agreed to help me. The youngest, in her twenties, responded: "I've decided to participate in your challenge. I'm interested to see the results of your experiment and what eye-opening things I can learn. Thanks for asking us."

My friends were so enthusiastic and so positive that I was overwhelmed, and I hoped they wouldn't be too disappointed at what they might, or might not, find out.

Now before I tell you what these women discovered through their three-day experiment, let me tell you of a woman who would never consider herself to be a holy woman. This woman would never think she moved through her life, through the normal activities of her days, in response to the question "What would a holy woman do?" Yet, read her son's account from an article in the July 2008 *Ensign* and decide for yourself.

A MOTHER'S EXAMPLE

First, a little background. This woman and her husband were concerned about the amount and quality of television programming that their sons watched. The following is what the oldest son wrote as he recalled an experience that made a significant difference in the spirit of their home.

"My brother and I were in front of the TV one Saturday night around midnight. . . . A tawdry comedy show that we shouldn't have been watching was on. The basement room was dark except for the light from the television. Without warning, Mother walked in. She was wearing a white, flowing nightgown and carrying a pair of shears. Making no sound, she reached behind the set, grabbed the cord, and gathered it into a loop. She then inserted the shears and cut the cord with a single stroke. Sparks flew and the set went dead, but not before Mother turned and glided out of the room."

Unnerved, [the eldest son] headed to bed. His innovative brother, however, cut a cord from a broken vacuum and connected it to the television. Soon the boys had plopped back down in front of the television, hardly missing any of their show.

"Mother, however, got the last laugh. . . . When we came home from school the next Monday, we found the television set in the middle of the floor with a huge crack through the thick glass screen. We immediately suspected Mother. When confronted, she responded with a perfectly straight face. 'I was dusting under the TV, and it slipped.'"

[Her husband] honored his wife's wishes, the children honored their mother's desires, and that was the end of television in [their] home. "For the most part, Mother leads through quiet example. . . . However, she is also inspired and fearless. Mother's assertiveness has been a great blessing to her children and grandchildren. Both in pivotal moments and in daily routines, she has forever changed the course of our lives." (Hales, *Ensign,* July 2008, 13–14)

Who was this fearless, holy woman? Sister Kathleen J. Eyring, wife of President Henry B. Eyring. Now I'm guessing that if Sister Eyring were here today, she would not say that you need to eliminate TV from your home. You don't have to take out your scissors and cut the cord or throw the television on the floor and crack the screen. You don't have to do any of that, but you might be surprised about what you *are* prompted to do when you view your concerns through the lens of the question "What would a holy woman do?"

HELEN

Now let's go back to my friends and the three-day experiment. On each of these three days, each woman was going to choose one daily activity—something she would normally do—but now she would do it as a holy woman would.

Let me tell you about the first woman. I'll call her Helen. Helen is a young wife and mother of two children, ages five and three, and she is eight months pregnant with her third child. What did she experience in those three days?

DAY ONE

On the very first morning, as she was lying in bed thinking about holiness, she became immediately intrigued with the power of such thinking because something occurred which she'd almost given up on after having tried everything the experts said. What miracle happened? Her three-year-old son came running into the bedroom and proudly announced that he was potty trained. A great start to any mother's day, but especially to that of a young mother who was just days away from giving birth to her third child!

A few hours later, as Helen took her children and dog for a walk, she started thinking about her visiting teaching appointment, which was scheduled for later in the day. She had been assigned as a visiting teacher to a new sister in the ward, and Helen was a little bit nervous. Everyone had warned her about the sister who, they said, was really quite stand-offish. But as Helen walked along the sidewalk, she started thinking, "How would a holy woman teach this sister?" Her heart started turning to this new sister, and Helen wondered how life looked from this woman's point of view. What might this sister be worried about? What might she need—really need?

Helen reported to me that usually when she prepares her visiting teaching lesson, she chooses one quote from the message. But, she said, that day *every quote in the visiting teaching message spoke to me, and I couldn't resist sharing each one of them with this sister.* She had a great experience visiting this new sister and teaching her. She couldn't believe how pleasant their time together was and how very different it was from what she had feared, simply because Helen had asked herself "How would a holy woman visit teach?"

DAY TWO

Helen hadn't initially decided on any activity in particular for the second day of the experiment. Then, suddenly, she knew what she wanted to do. She wanted to read her scriptures. So Helen started reading. "That's a holy woman kind of thing to do," she thought. Just as she started reading, though, her children interrupted her. What does a holy woman do then? Helen knew. A holy woman would be with her children.

Helen thought, "Well, if I'm going to be with my children, I'm *really* going to *be with* them." So she decided she would play a game with them—a new game. It was several weeks after Christmas and she knew right where a brand-new board game was. It had never been opened. Helen patiently took each playing piece out of the box, one by one, and slowly and carefully read the directions for the game. All of this took quite a long time, but Helen patiently persisted. Suddenly, her five-year-old daughter turned to Helen and said, "Mom, this is the *first* day I *really* love."

"What do you mean?" asked Helen.

"We get to be with you."

"What do you mean? I'm *always* here with you," Helen protested.

"No, you're not," countered her daughter. "We're in our rooms playing, and you're always working somewhere else in the house. But today—today, we get to play with you. We really get to *be with* you. This is the first day I really love."

Wow! When Helen relayed that story to me, I was so overwhelmed by the truths her little five-year-old girl had spoken that I forgot to ask Helen about her third day. However, Helen did tell me the practice she followed for those three days: She prayed three times a day specifically about holiness—once in the morning to be a holy woman, then during a particular activity so she would know how a holy woman would do it, and then at night when she gave thanks to the Lord for helping her to understand more about being a holy woman.

LESSONS LEARNED

So what did Helen learn from those three days? She said, "I learned that desiring to be holy brings changes." Helen was amazed with the changes. Her productivity increased. Her energy increased. She wasn't tired, even though she was eight months pregnant, and she wanted to exercise and clean her home.

Helen e-mailed me several days after we talked. She wrote, "I asked my husband if he noticed a difference in me over those three days and he said, 'Yes, one day you were *really nice* to me!' So, I've learned a lot about myself over these three days. I've learned that I need to spend more time with my children when I can really focus on them and not be multitasking with them in the background. And I learned that I need to be nicer to my husband."

JULIE

L et me tell you of another woman—Julie. She's a mother of four children, ages two through ten. Julie said she wanted to try the experiment and apply it to tasks that were *really* troublesome for her as a mother. What did she do?

DAY ONE

Julia chose brushing her four-year-old daughter's teeth. This was typically a major trauma which often led to a total meltdown for both mother and daughter. But on this day when Julie asked herself "What would a holy woman do?" she pictured the Savior being in the room with her. She had more patience. She didn't bark orders. Julie said, "I didn't feel so out of control.

I saw the situation rationally and asked myself 'How would a holy woman handle this situation?' I enjoyed my daughter and the brushing of her teeth, which went more quickly than ever before."

DAY TWO

Julie chose to focus on how to prevent her children from arguing with each other. What would a holy woman do? That question guided Julie as she helped her children through the activities of the day. She said it was a most remarkable day. She reported, "I seemed to have had more ability to solve problems. There were no escalating emotions. No runaway-train experiences. Even going shopping with my children in tow, which is usually such a high-stress experience, was not. I felt more capable, more creative. I had more influence with my children. I could step back and see the situation for what it was and then teach them how to solve the problem or how to act. I kept thinking, 'Hey, I can do this!' and that's a new thought for me."

DAY THREE

Julie chose to focus on her Church calling in her ward; she serves in Young Women. On that particular day, she and another sister had been assigned to clean out the Young Women closet at the chapel. "Not very inspiring," Julie thought. "But what would a holy woman do?" That question helped Julie. Julie is a highly creative woman with very little patience for the mundane, but that day she found herself being more patient while doing the tasks. Her appreciation for the other woman increased as they worked together, and Julie found herself energized with the feeling of being more capable than she sometimes felt she was.

LESSONS LEARNED

What did Julie learn from those three days? She said, "I now know that being holy is not an unreachable goal. I can be more holy every day. I initially wanted to do more than one thing a day, but having only one thing to do really helped me to focus. Working on being holy helped me feel like a more capable, better person."

CAROL

Carol is a wife and a mother of three little girls all under the age of nine. Her husband is busy both professionally and with Church callings. Two days prior to me offering Carol this experiment, she was making some New Year's resolutions. She was wondering how to improve her life.

Carol is a very organized woman able to juggle many things at once and do them all really well. Her days were already tightly scheduled, and she admitted to me that she couldn't imagine adding one more thing to her life. Yet, for all the good things she was accomplishing in a day, she could feel that some things were missing. She knew there were people who got up an hour earlier in order to add more to their days, however, she also knew *she* couldn't do that. "I knew I would just be more tired during the day," she said. "I know my limit."

For three days Carol asked herself "What would a holy woman do?" and she followed through on the ideas that came to her. And what changed? She was still able to do all the things she normally did within her tightly planned schedule—plus more. For example, when it was time on her schedule to exercise, she exercised—but this time she listened to inspirational talks on CD. Later she found she was able to use information from the CDs when talking to a friend in distress. Another example: When it was time for Carol to eat breakfast after everyone was finally out the door, she read the *Ensign* while she ate. Another example: When it was time to get ready for the day, she did so while listening to the Book of Mormon on CD. Her five-year-old daughter joined her, bringing her own scriptures into her parents' room and following along as the Book of Mormon CD played.

LESSONS LEARNED

What difference did asking that important question make for Carol? She said, "When I asked myself the question 'What would a holy woman do?' I was able to focus. More things got done and my priorities were good." And what did Carol learn through that three-day experiment? Here are Carol's own words: "Thinking about being holy gives purpose to your life and to your activities. Holiness means exercising faith—continually *desiring* faith. Faith is knowing why I do what I do. Christ is real."

MARILYN

Marilyn also accepted the invitation in my e-mail. Here are a few highlights of her three days. First, Marilyn said that one day as she spoke with a friend, the question "What would a holy woman do?" kept coming to her mind. Marilyn said that the question prompted her to be very careful about the topics they covered. And then she added, "There was absolutely no gossiping."

Marilyn experienced an unusual ability to recall significant events and concerns in her friend's life and knew useful questions to ask to help her friend see her same old problems in a new way. Trying to be holy invited the Spirit into Marilyn's conversations, and she loved that.

Another highlight was the very personal, memorable

reassurances which Marilyn received from the Lord regarding the relentless activities related to her mothering. As the mother of several young children, Marilyn was often overwhelmed with the intensive, seemingly never-ending, physical care of her children. Even with her background as a nurse, she felt she was always running and barely keeping up with daily demands.

Marilyn said, "If I kneel to pray, I have little children crawling on my back. If I close the door, they knock. And who knows what disaster I'll come out to. Mothering is hard. Some days all I can read are five *verses* of scriptures. That's it." Marilyn choked up several times as she described to me the contrasting calm and very unexpected reassurances she felt which let her know that her children's physical care really *was* important and, in fact, was *exactly* what she needed to be doing as a holy woman in this particular time in her life.

LESSONS LEARNED

Knowing that the Lord knew her heart and her desire to focus on things that Marilyn considered to be "more spiritual—more holy" moved her to tears over and over again as we talked. She felt sanctioned by the Lord about what she *was* doing, and her guilt about all she thought she *wasn't* doing fell away. Marilyn felt acknowledged by the Lord and supported by Him in her mothering. What a blessing this was for this great mother!

Another highlight for Marilyn was the words which kept coming to her mind when she thought about being more holy. Each word started with the letter P: perspective, patience, perseverance, and plan.

Perspective? Marilyn said, "I could see my children's needs in an entirely new light." Patience? She said, "Discipline and teaching replaced my grouchiness with the children." Perseverance? She said, "Even the repetitiveness of cleaning my floors suddenly seemed like a holy thing to do." Plan? "Planning just one thing to do with the children each day really changed the franticness I felt before."

What else did Marilyn learn? Three other things stood out for her. She said, "I learned that I don't need to lose my temper just because things are spiraling out of control. I noticed things about my children I hadn't been noticing before, like how there are moments when they actually play well together. And I learned that being holy doesn't mean being perfect."

KATE

Now let me tell you of a young wife and a mother of an almost one-year-old boy. On the first day of the experiment, Kate chose shopping as the thing she wanted to do as a holy woman. She anticipated all of the negative messages on the covers of the magazines at the checkout counter. What would a holy woman do? Kate was prepared. She would focus on her baby boy, and she did. But even so, the longer she stood in line, the easier it was to let her eyes wander. She couldn't believe how the negative messages of the world were *everywhere.* She realized how easily she could be distracted from her goal to be more holy, and she realized how strong the pull of the world was. She was so distressed by her experiences at the checkout counter that, upon her return home, she and her husband talked for a long time and developed a plan about how they could keep the negative influences of the world out of their home and out of their minds and hearts.

DAY TWO

On day two, Kate focused on her negative responses to her husband's evening meetings. She realized she had drifted into a pattern of complaining, both verbally and non-verbally, about her husband needing to leave home some nights to serve in his calling as elders' quorum president.

Kate said she would guilt-trip him. "I wouldn't make eye contact with my husband or I would glare. I had several ways of letting him know just how unhappy I was that *he* was going out and that *I* was once again going to be left alone with our baby boy." Evenings were their son's cranky time and, when her husband was gone, they were Kate's cranky time too!

When Kate asked herself the question "What would a holy woman do?" she was flooded with ideas. She suddenly wanted to support her husband and not make him feel guilty. In fact, she had a memory flashback to her mother's wise counsel taught years earlier, when Kate was just a young woman: "Never make your husband feel guilty for fulfilling his church callings." Wow! Kate had forgotten that advice entirely.

LESSONS LEARNED

Kate realized that she could plan what she and her baby would do while her husband was away. For example, she could plan teaching and learning games with her son. Kate followed through on several ideas she had, and she could not believe what happened:

- She was patient with her son.
- She enjoyed him so much more.
- She saw her baby as a child of God and when he became cranky, she looked at that moment as a privilege—an opportunity to cuddle him and comfort him like no one else could.

What a change! Kate was also more productive when her son was sleeping. She even felt like mopping her floors or organizing a closet. There was no time to wallow, and Kate said, "My husband came home to a wife with a far happier disposition."

TAKE A MOMENT
TO REFLECT

As you've considered these women's experiences, what has the Spirit taught you? Can you take a moment and write down any impressions you have had? Are there things you want to start doing? Things you want to stop doing? If you would like, take a few moments to write down your thoughts and feelings.

WHAT WOULD A HOLY WOMAN DO?

_____

_____

_____

_____

_____

_____

_____

_____

_____

_____

_____

_____

_____

_____

_____

_____

_____

_____

_____

_____

_____

BARBARA

Now let me tell you about a few more women and their experiences. Let me tell you about Barbara, age sixty-five—wife, mother, grandmother. Thinking about being a holier woman helped her in several situations. She was so excited about all that happened in only one day that she e-mailed me about the positive influence the question had had on her life at the end of day one.

Here's what Barbara said: "I wasn't critical of my husband, and didn't make any snide comments when he was driving. This was important for me. I bit my tongue and realized that my comments were so unnecessary. I had a huge realization that people are trying to do the best they can."

She continued, "The question also helped me when I was ironing my husband's shirt and a button came off. Rather than putting the shirt in a pile for a week or two, I found myself wanting to put the button back on right now. This may seem like a little thing, but for me it wasn't. Procrastination has been a problem of mine, but when I think about what a holy woman would do, procrastination is not the answer. Doing things promptly is. The question also helped me with my eating. I think a woman who is trying to be more holy would be more selective about what she puts in her mouth. I believe a holy woman would exercise and try to keep healthy. This question has been on my mind almost continually all day long and has influenced my actions many times in only one day."

Well, that was quite a day for Barbara! She is a great woman who is always eager to improve, and she is open to feedback—especially when brought to her by the Holy Ghost.

CAROLYN

I had an opportunity to share the experiences of these six women with a group of women in an eastern state of the USA. I extended to those women the same three-day experiment, and I appreciated the insights of one great young mother. She has been married for eight years and has three children—ages six, four, and two. Let's call her Carolyn. Carolyn e-mailed me the following note. Here is what she wrote:

> Dear Sister Nelson,
>
> Your challenge for me personally was timely in that I've thought very seriously recently about making permanent and lasting changes in becoming more righteous and

steadfast. My first thought in trying to become a more holy woman was "Where do I begin?" There are so many rough spots that need to be buffed out. How do I possibly pick one?

When I came home from the Women's Conference that night it was obvious where I had to begin. My first small challenge came from my four-year-old. Of the three of my children, he has always been more sensitive and more easily set-off than the other two. That night he wanted something I couldn't find. In order to calm him I practiced "active listening," just like my professors taught me. Then I thought, "How would a holy woman handle this situation? Would she practice active listening just to quiet a child down, or would she do something different?"

I determined that it was inappropriate to use active listening on my child and instead tried to lovingly listen and counsel with the Spirit on how to best reassure him. I told my son that I didn't know where the lost items were and that first thing in the morning I would help him find them, but if I found them before, I would give them to him. My son felt reassured, and when I did find what he wanted, I promptly gave them to him.

What magnificent insights were brought to this young mother by the Holy Ghost! The Spirit helped Carolyn discern that in her particular mothering moment, active listening—which may be useful in some situations—was not the way to help her son.

Can you see how eager the Lord is to personally and specifically tutor us in our very hour of need—even in our very *moment* of need? All we need to do is ask.

SISTERS AROUND THE WORLD

When I had the privilege of meeting with some of our Russian sisters, I offered them the same three-day challenge. I received the following e-mail reporting the experiences of several of our Russian sisters.

Galina said, "This time I tried to serve my sister as a holy woman. It has brought surprising feelings of love and pleasure."

Svetlana reported, "I have decided to keep my thoughts and words pure, to tell my point of view without criticizing another, to show more mercy. This week I have tried to show more gratitude, especially to my family. I've tried to help an elderly employee more and not pay attention to her strange behavior. When I witnessed a quarrel between my daughter and her husband, I told both of them how strongly I love them. It helped them to settle the conflict."

Tatiana reported, "I have decided that a holy woman would be pure in everything—in actions, words, thoughts, and desires. I tried to keep my home clean, to put each thing in its place, to finish something when I start it. This approach lets me spend so much less time putting my home in order. Next I had a feeling of pleasure and joy. Also, I've tried to find something good in each person with whom I communicate. This was a miracle. I was surprised how blessed each of us are. I saw new aspects of people whom I've known for years—aspects I've never seen before. I've been amazed by the richness and uniqueness of their souls. My soul was filled with joy. I also wanted to create beauty around me in spite of the fact that I live alone. My children have grown already, but I set the table with candles every night this week. It has given me the sensation of living in a fairy story."

A woman in Canada tried the three-day challenge and e-mailed me the following letter:

As I suspected it would, this challenge began as a confirmation of how far off the mark I generally fall. What I did not suspect was how easy it was to have that question firmly planted in my brain. It is well past the three days and I still hear it.

At first I had the wording all wrong. Instead of asking myself what a holy woman would do, I chastised myself saying, "That's not what a holy woman would do" or "A holy woman would not raise her voice to get her children to hurry up so that they could be on time for church." Frustration set in, and I realized how negative wording rapidly led to negative results. I resolved to turn things around.

I tried to hold my tongue when complaints arose. I had a dose of what I try to teach my children—I wasn't to complain but to search for a solution. Other highlights include:

- I stole moments to just look at my children and admire the extraordinary people they are—which inevitably led to extra hugs and cuddles.
- Instead of clashing with my very like-minded four-year-old daughter—we played.

I am much more fun when not consumed by my to-do list, and since a holy woman would put her four-year-old at the top of her list, that's what I did. All she wants is my time and she got much more of it when I ensured that my computer remained turned off and the answering machine was put to work. Her behavior improved with the extra attention, and we were both happier.

- In a moment of quiet, which I was able to notice without the distraction of my computer and phone, I picked up the *Ensign*. After unwrapping it (sigh), I enjoyed an entire article before I was called on by my children.

- I got more sleep! I am typically not in bed at a decent hour but a holy woman would follow the adage "early to bed, early to rise," and I must say, I enjoyed it. It also made the following day so much easier to enjoy. It never ceases to amaze me that although I know that's how it works I so often fail to make sleep a priority.

- I made time to pray. One of my biggest shortcomings is that I often convince myself that Heavenly Father has more important children with bigger problems to listen to. It has been lovely to remind myself that I am worth His time. A holy woman knows it.

- A holy woman is so much more at peace with herself and her surroundings. I liked myself more, I enjoyed my children more, and I appreciated moments more. I kept myself busy admiring the lovely shade of grass on my side of the fence.

Thank you for issuing the three-day challenge. My competitive nature ensured my participation. Now the trick is to re-challenge myself on a regular basis. I struggle in many areas and have been feeling spiritually deflated for quite some time. This challenge is helping me.

EXTENDING THE INVITATION TO FAMILY MEMBERS

I t seems that other family members may also be eager to learn about holiness. One mother wrote:

> Yesterday we were driving down the high-
> way and I put in your CD about what a holy
> woman would do and started to listen. The kids
> were actually quiet and also listened to it—the
> entire way to our destination! When the CD
> finished, Joseph (age six years) asked me, "Mom,
> does Wendy have a CD that tells me what a holy
> boy would do?" Well, what a smart fellow he is!
> I told him that the things he heard, he could do
> in *his* life, too! So this morning, when the kids
> started quarreling over the markers they use
> to draw pictures, Joseph stood up and said to

them, "This is not what a holy boy would do! A holy boy would not yell!" And then they shared the markers and didn't yell anymore. In fact, right now they are quietly making masterpieces in the other room for their daddy.

A young man in Brazil took the three-day challenge and this is his report, originally written in Portuguese:

I wanted to thank you for the opportunity to report what I did as a holy young man for these three days. One day the activity that I chose to do was to play volleyball. I was patient when we lost a point, and I tried to give my best for the team. We ended up winning against the team with the two teachers! Another day I helped some friends of mine that had difficulties.

I want to let you know that I felt much more holy, and wish to continue doing this every day.

With care,
Gabriel

WHAT AWAITS YOU?

Now, what is the Lord willing to teach *you* about holiness? If, for just three days, you took the holy woman challenge, what would you learn? If, for just three days, you chose an activity, something you already do—just one activity each day—and ask yourself the question "How would a holy woman do this? What would a holy woman do?"—what would you be drawn to do? How different would your days unfold if, in a difficult situation, you asked yourself "What would a holy woman do?"

In section 46 of the Doctrine and Covenants, the Lord makes it clear that He is serious about us learning about holiness. He says in verse 33, "Ye *must* practice . . . holiness before me" (emphasis added). He doesn't leave it at that. He adds the word *continually.* Imagine. The Lord *commands* us to practice holiness before him *continually.* Does that sound like the Lord wants us to learn holiness? That He wants us to be more holy? But how? How can we do it?

We can't do it on our own. We can't be holy on our own. We can't practice holiness on our own, and we are not supposed to. The Lord's command to practice holiness before Him continually is the very last verse in section 46. What proceeds that verse? Verses 7 through 12 in Section 46 command us to ask God for gifts of the Spirit which can help us become more holy. And verses 13 through 26 enumerate some of the gifts of the Spirit which can help us in our earnest seeking of holiness. (Other gifts of the Spirit are listed in Moroni 10 and in 1 Corinthians 12–14.)

Have you noticed that when the Lord places the same truth in three different books of scripture, it's a pretty good indication that that particular truth is really important to the Lord? Gifts of the Spirit are really important to Him. Our seeking for gifts of the Spirit is really important to Him.

One more question: Are the gifts which are listed

in those three scriptural sources *all* of the gifts of the Spirit available to help us? No. Absolutely not! Elder Bruce R. McConkie taught that the gifts listed in those three sources are only suggestions, only the beginning of possible gifts available (see *Mormon Doctrine,* 314–15). Elder McConkie also taught, "These gifts are infinite in number and endless in their manifestations because God himself is infinite and endless" (*New Witness for the Articles of Faith,* 270).

Now for some more great news. In Doctrine and Covenants 60:7 the Lord says very clearly, "I am able to make you holy." Think of that truth. *He is able to make us holy.* How comforting is that? How encouraging! How invigorating! And He will. So what do we need to do? What's our part?

First, we need to let the Lord know that we're serious about becoming more holy. And then what?

GIFTS OF THE SPIRIT
AND HOLINESS

Many people love to give gifts (and many more love to receive them), and a popular trend in gift gifting is the "gift card."

A gift card can be a great idea. Perhaps your friend lives far away from you and the cost of shipping may outweigh the cost of the gift, or perhaps you don't know quite what your friend might really want or need, or what size she wears, or the date and time she may have available to use a service you are purchasing for her.

Because of the Savior's infinite Atonement, we have access to spiritual gifts. The Savior has paid the price for all the gifts of the Spirit you will ever need in your life and throughout all eternity! And He paid an infinite price for those gifts, which are "endowments of godly traits" (Callister, *Infinite Atonement,* 268).

Think of it this way: the Savior has paid for a monumental, never ending number of spiritual gift cards—so to speak—just for you!

Metaphorically, these spiritual gift cards were given to you when you received the gift of the Holy Ghost as you were confirmed a member of The Church of Jesus Christ of Latter-day Saints.

The *gift* (singular) of the Holy Ghost gives you access to the *gifts* (plural) of the Holy Ghost. The Holy Ghost can deliver the spiritual gifts to you upon your diligent, even desperate, seeking.

What if you are ready to use one of your spiritual gift cards but you don't know which one to use?

Pray about that dilemma.

Some of our most important prayers are when we pray to know what to pray about! So, pray and listen.

And now, let me tell you of one of the main downfalls of gift cards: some people never use them.

I have had one gift card for almost seven years. I forgot about it for about three years, then I lost it for another two years, then I found it again, but I still haven't used it. Let's not be like that when it comes to our spiritual gift cards. Let's use them to obtain the spiritual gifts we need. Use them eagerly. Persistently.

What spiritual gifts may help you to become more holy? Well, actually, any gift that will help you with a weakness can do that.

You and I know our own personal weaknesses.

We know the temptations that keep tripping us up.

We know the weaknesses of the natural woman that can cause us trouble—lots of trouble.

We know, as Paul said so well, "the sins which do so easily beset us" (Hebrews 12:1).

So, pray to know which particular spiritual gift would counteract one of your weaknesses. What spiritual gift would actually turn that weakness into a strength?

Pray to know.

Here are some examples:

- If you're too negative with your children, your friends, or your spouse, ask for the gift of hope, of optimism.

- If you lose your temper and are cruel in what you say to those you love, ask for the gift of mildness or understanding.

- If you have started the same diet every Monday for the past three years and are still overweight, ask for the gift of self-discipline. Or the gift to be healed. Ask for the gift of peace so that anxiety, fear, frustration, and fatigue will no longer drive you to the fridge or to the fast food pick-up window.

- If you've never been able to keep your home tidy and clean—and you know that the Holy Ghost enjoys a clean environment—ask for the gift of self-discipline. Perhaps the gift of better time management or the gift of discernment would help so that you are spending your time on things that really matter.

- If you are easily discouraged, pray for the spiritual gift of persistence. Of endurance.

- If you find that you are increasingly anxious about many things, ask for the gift of peace. His peace surpasseth *all* understanding and cuts through the fear of *every* situation.

- If you are shy and have never been very good at reaching out to others, pray for the gift of listening, even discernment, so you can really hear and know what is in someone's heart.

- If you are easily hurt by others, pray for the gift of faith. Faith in the Lord Jesus Christ is a spiritual gift that will be a shield to you against the unkind words and actions of others.

- If life has always been pretty easy for you, and you've always been the best and the brightest, pray for the gift of humility and for the ability to learn from everyone you meet—and I mean *everyone.*

What are some other gifts that may help you in your quest to increase in holiness?

- The gift of a cheerful countenance so that people are drawn to you. (You can actually pray for that!)

- The gift of true conversion so that nothing—and I mean *nothing*—can distract you or dissuade you from living the truths of the restored gospel of Jesus Christ.

- The gift of selflessness.
- The gift of forgiveness.
- The gift to be healed.
- The gift of wisdom—even the wisdom of angels.

Now, will a casual prayer or a casual presentation of your gift card—so to speak—to your Heavenly Father be enough for you to acquire the spiritual gift you are seeking? Never! Zero chance!

Listen to the words of Elder Tad R. Callister, author of *The Infinite Atonement*.

> Mormon knew that a casual request would never suffice [in obtaining spiritual gifts]. Speaking of the gift of charity, he said that we must "pray unto the Father with all the energy of heart, that ye may be filled with this love" (Moroni 7:48). . . . Pure obedience and silent endurance are not enough. (*Infinite Atonement,* 274)

That last sentence and this next one always catch my attention and take my breath away.

Elder Callister continues:

There must be a burning desire, a reaching out, a seeking, in short, an exhaustive exercise of our combined spiritual, intellectual, and emotional energies, all focused on obtaining these divine gifts. (*Infinite Atonement,* 274)*

And as Elder Russell M. Nelson wisely taught, "We can acquire holiness only by enduring and persistent personal effort" (*Ensign,* May 2001, 32). Start by praying for one specific gift that will help you with one specific weakness. Ask for it. Plead for it. Fast for it. Then pray for another gift to help with another weakness. And then another, and another. Gift upon gift, you and I can become more holy.

---

* I would also encourage you to prayerfully and repeatedly study chapter 23, "The Blessing of Grace," in *The Infinite Atonement* by Elder Tad R. Callister for further insights that will increase your desire to seek and your desire to be more holy.

AS WE SEEK TO INCREASE
IN HOLINESS

I pray that we will seek to be more holy—that we will ask ourselves in many different, and even difficult, situations, "What would a holy woman do?" and then notice what the Spirit of the Lord teaches us. I pray that we will then follow through on those teachings. I pray that we will seek the spiritual gifts that will increase our holiness.

I know that because of the Savior's infinite Atonement, those gifts are right there, waiting to help us become more holy. With enduring and persistent personal effort we can access the particular gifts of the Spirit that we so desperately need. Through this process we truly can become a little more holy today than yesterday and a little more holy tomorrow than we are today.

I pray that each time we enter the temple and we see the words, "Holiness to the Lord," we will feel joy knowing we are doing our part to *bring* holiness to the Lord, to the House of the Lord.

I have been drawn to the words and music of "Lord, Make Us a Holy People" by Victoria Wilcox. You may enjoy downloading the sheet music at http://deseretbook.com/pdf/Lord_Make_Us_Holy_People .pdf and singing this song with those you love.

LORD, MAKE US A HOLY PEOPLE

Words and music by Victoria Wilcox

Oh, Lord, make us a holy people.
Lord, show us the way.
That we may be thy Saints forever
And serve thee each day.
For Zion is the pure in heart;
Purify us, we pray,
That we may be a holy people
Who covenant and obey.

Oh Savior, let thy sweet forgiveness,
Grace lovingly giv'n
Free us from the bonds that bind us;
Wash clean all our sins.
Oh, Savior, let thy spirit send
Blessings from above.
Oh, Lord, make us a holy people,
And worthy to share thy love.

Oh, Lord, sanctify all our efforts in thy holy name.
That when we come at last before thee,
Thy presence we'll claim
For we would be the pure in heart.
Zion come among men.
Oh, Lord make us a holy people
That we may be called thy friends.

BIBLIOGRAPHY

Callister, Tad R. *The Infinite Atonement.* Salt Lake City: Deseret Book, 2000.

Hales, Robert D. "President Henry B. Eyring: Called of God," *Ensign,* July 2008, 8–15.

McConkie, Bruce R. *Mormon Doctrine,* 2d ed. Salt Lake City: Bookcraft, 1966.

———. *A New Witness for the Articles of Faith.* Salt Lake City: Deseret Book, 1985.

Nelson, Russell M. "Personal Preparation for Temple Blessings," *Ensign,* May 32–35.

I INVITE YOU TO TRY THE
THREE-DAY EXPERIMENT:
"WHAT WOULD A HOLY WOMAN DO?"

BEGINNING THOUGHTS

_____

_____

_____

_____

_____

_____

_____

_____

_____

_____

DAY ONE

_____

_____

_____

_____

_____

_____

_____

_____

_____

_____

_____

_____

_____

_____

_____

_____

DAY TWO

_____

_____

_____

_____

_____

_____

_____

_____

_____

_____

_____

_____

_____

_____

_____

_____

DAY THREE

LESSONS LEARNED

_____

_____

_____

_____

_____

_____

_____

_____

_____

_____

_____

_____

_____

_____

_____